ANIMAL TRAINER

BY PATRICK PERISH

BELLWETHER MEDIA · MINNEAPOLIS, MN

Are you ready to take it to the extreme?
Torque books thrust you into the action-packed world
of sports, vehicles, mystery, and adventure. These books
may include dirt, smoke, fire, and dangerous stunts.
WARNING: read at your own risk.

Library of Congress Cataloging-in-Publication Data

Perish, Patrick, author.
  Animal Trainer / by Patrick Perish.
      pages cm. -- (Torque. Dangerous Jobs)
  Includes bibliographical references and index.
  Summary: "Engaging images accompany information about animal trainers. The combination of
high-interest subject matter and light text is intended for students in grades 3 through 7"-- Provided
by publisher.
  Audience: Ages 7-12.
  ISBN 978-1-62617-196-1 (hardcover : alk. paper)
  1. Animal training--Vocational guidance--Juvenile literature. 2. Animal trainers--Juvenile literature. I.
Title. II. Series: Dangerous Jobs (Minneapolis, Minn.)
  GV1829.P45 2015
  636.08'35--dc23
                                     2014034780

This edition first published in 2015 by Bellwether Media, Inc.

Printed in the United States of America, North Mankato, MN.

TABLE OF CONTENTS

CHAPTER 1

TIGER ATTACK!

The audience buzzes with excitement. An animal trainer stands in the center of the stage. He is performing tricks with a tiger. Everything is going well. Suddenly, the big cat growls. It jumps toward the trainer.

The trainer reacts quickly. He distracts the tiger with his **taming stick**. Other trainers rush to help. They safely put the tiger in its cage. The show is over, but the trainers and the crowd are safe.

Take a Seat

Animal trainers for the circus sometimes use chairs to control big cats. The many legs of a chair confuse the animals.

CHAPTER 2

ANIMAL TRAINERS

Animal trainers teach animals to follow commands and be comfortable around people. Trainers work with many animals to perform different tasks. They might teach animals to perform **stunts** in circuses, act in movies, or work as service animals. Others work in pet stores and at zoos.

Horsing Around

Some trainers work with police horses. They train the horses how to respond to loud noises and other things that usually spook them.

Trainers must decide if an animal is a good fit for a job. Every animal behaves differently. Trainers give animals rewards for good behaviors. They often give the animals food or playtime. One of the first things they teach is **hygiene** training. Trained animals need to cooperate for regular checkups.

Good Patients

Elephants lift their feet and open their mouths for cleaning. Orcas hold still for blood tests.

The Deep End

Animal trainers who work at water parks need to be excellent swimmers and divers.

Trainers are experts on the animal **species** they train. Many of them study **biology** in college. Then they learn from other trainers on the job. They end up with experiences with a variety of animals.

CHAPTER 3

DANGER!

Animal trainers face many **hazards** on the job. Animals, especially wild ones, are **unpredictable**. They can be trained to perform, but they never lose their **instincts**. Surprises such as flashing lights and loud noises can spook animals into attacking.

At zoos, animals are used to seeing visitors and trainers every day. Many look very comfortable around people. Still, the animals are dangerous. Sick or injured animals might not behave as expected during **routine** cleaning or feeding. Animals that are **harassed** by visitors might defend themselves.

Attack Count

There were at least 17 animal attacks in water parks and zoos in the United States between 2000 and 2010.

Even working with **domesticated** animals can be risky. Animals such as horses and dogs have been raised to be friendly. However, friendly animals can become dangerous when they feel **threatened**. Animals that have not been properly **socialized** might get scared or become **aggressive**.

Trainers know that animals can be dangerous, but to them the risks are worth it. They feel a deep connection with the animal world. That connection inspires them to take on the challenge of animal training. Above all, trainers care about showing that animals are intelligent and deserve respect.

Tragedy on the Job

On February 24, 2010, trainer Dawn Brancheau drowned during a SeaWorld show in Orlando, Florida. An orca named Tilikum grabbed her ponytail and pulled her underwater.

Glossary

aggressive—ready to attack

biology—the study of living things

domesticated—kept as a pet or on a farm

harassed—teased in an unkind way

hazards—risks of harm or loss

hygiene—practices that keep an animal clean and healthy

instincts—natural behaviors or skills

routine—performed on a regular basis

socialized—taught to behave well with others

species—animal groups; a species of animals has one name and many shared characteristics.

stunts—difficult or dangerous feats

taming stick—a pole used by animal trainers to communicate with animals

threatened—to feel at risk

unpredictable—having behavior that is hard or impossible to guess

To Learn More

AT THE LIBRARY

Grayson, Robert. *Performers*. New York, N.Y.: Marshall Cavendish Benchmark, 2011.

Koehler, Susan. *Animal Trainer*. Vero Beach, Fla.: Rourke, 2010.

Miller, Connie Colwell. *Movie Animals*. Mankato, Minn.: Amicus High Interest, 2014.

ON THE WEB

Learning more about animal trainers is as easy as 1, 2, 3.

1. Go to www.factsurfer.com.

2. Enter "animal trainers" into the search box.

3. Click the "Surf" button and you will see a list of related web sites.

With factsurfer.com, finding more information is just a click away.

Index